LEAR
Capello

Also by Tim Bradford:

Is Shane MacGowan Still Alive?

The Groundwater Diaries

Acknowledgements

Many thanks to David North, who supports Everton and also enjoys watching football, for coming up with the idea of writing *Learn to Speak Capello*.

Further Reading

Calcio: A History of Italian Football, John Foot, Fourth Estate, 2006; *Forza Italia: The Fall and Rise of Italian Football*, Paddy Agnew, Ebury, 2006; *A Season with Verona*, Tim Parks, Secker & Warburg, 2002; *Complete Book of the World Cup*, Cris Freddi, HarperCollins, 2006

LEARN TO SPEAK
Capello

Tim Bradford

Italian translations by
Clara Furlan and Jon Hunt

First published 2008 by Boxtree
an imprint of Pan Macmillan Ltd
Pan Macmillan, 20 New Wharf Road, London N1 9RR
Basingstoke and Oxford
Associated companies throughout the world
www.panmacmillan.com

ISBN 978-0-7522-2677-4

Copyright © Tim Bradford 2008
Italian translation © Clara Furlan and Jon Hunt 2008

The right of Tim Bradford to be identified as the
author of this work has been asserted by him in accordance
with the Copyright, Designs and Patents Act 1988.

All rights reserved. No part of this publication may be
reproduced, stored in or introduced into a retrieval system, or
transmitted, in any form, or by any means (electronic, mechanical,
photocopying, recording or otherwise) without the prior written
permission of the publisher. Any person who does any unauthorized
act in relation to this publication may be liable to criminal
prosecution and civil claims for damages.

1 3 5 7 9 8 6 4 2

A CIP catalogue record for this book is available from
the British Library.

Printed and bound in the UK by
CPI Mackays, Chatham, ME5 8TD

This book is sold subject to the condition that it shall not,
by way of trade or otherwise, be lent, re-sold, hired out,
or otherwise circulated without the publisher's prior consent
in any form of binding or cover other than that in which
it is published and without a similar condition including this
condition being imposed on the subsequent purchaser.

Visit **www.panmacmillan.com** to read more about all our books
and to buy them. You will also find features, author interviews and
news of any author events, and you can sign up for e-newsletters
so that you're always first to hear about our new releases.

Introduction

Fabio Capello coming to manage England is a bit like Lou Reed coming out of retirement to join McFly. He's done it all and you wonder: does he really need the hassle of hanging out with lesser mortals? But Capello must have seen something in the honest kick-and-hoof antics of John T, Stevey G, Frank and the gang; something he liked enough to risk his reputation and leave behind the comfort of home for the celebrity- and instant-success-fixated UK.

Maybe we're all seriously flattered that he wants to manage our team. Let's be honest, most of us had never heard of Sven before he came to England, but Capello is a legend. Has he fully understood the list of managers who have crashed and burned since Sir Alf was sacked by the FA thirty-five years ago? Don Revie, Graham Taylor, Glenn Hoddle, Kevin Keegan, Steve McClaren . . . And that's not counting the ones hounded out of office for alleged financial irregularities, or whose hair was turned white overnight by the constant media pressure.

Maybe Fabio Capello coming to manage England is more like Robert De Niro in his prime leaving Hollywood to take up a regular job on *Coronation Street*; it's more comedy than drama these days, but everyone will be watching. And maybe Fabio will manage to get over the English obsession with passion. Passion to us means being able to shout and point at the same time and then losing your temper.

My editor Jon Butler contacted me saying he wanted to publish a spoof Italian guide to coincide with Don Fabio's first competitive match against the mighty Andorra. I don't speak Italian, but Jon had access to two excellent Italian translators, Clara Furlan and Jon Hunt, and knew my writing and cartoons about football from *When Saturday Comes* and the *Guardian*. Over a couple of pints one night we somehow managed to fuse our interests into this one exciting project. We hope that if you ever get offered a job managing a Serie A side it will come in handy (yes, that includes you, Sam Allardyce).

I got a bit of insight into the sophistication of Italian fan culture during the 1990 World Cup when it seemed everyone from infant to great-grandparent had their own theories about tactics and personnel. And my own experience of the Italian football team is probably fairly typical of the English football fan: I've both hated and loved them, felt sorry for them, been frustrated by them and occasionally laughed at them.

I'm writing this on the night that Spain have just won the European Championships playing football as it is supposed to be played – high tempo, great technique, good movement, slick angles, quick passing, bright little midfielders scurrying about cleverly avoiding more muscular, clumsy opponents, great hair. For so long Spain were like us – a dormant football force, massive underachievers in international football. Now that title is no longer shared.

Alas, England still play with the muscularity of Germany without the cohesion and success; yet still have that shoot-in-foot ability that Spain had without the great technique or the Alice bands. So, a bit of work to do then.

But maybe, just maybe, Fabio Capello coming to manage England is a bit like the Man With No Name coming to a helpless Mexican village and helping them defeat the evil bandits by teaching them how they can help themselves.

Welcome to our world, Fabio.

Module One
Modulo Uno

At Home
A Casa

Fabio is in the garden.
Fabio è in giardino.

Fabio is sitting in the garden.
Fabio è seduto in giardino.

Fabio is sitting in the garden, contemplating the later works of Kandinsky and the escalation of the international art market.
Fabio è seduto in giardino a contemplare le opere tarde di Kandinsky e la crescita del mercato internazionale dell'arte.

Grandpa Trapattoni is asleep in the atrium with his trophies.
Nonno Trapattoni sta dormendo nell'atrio con i suoi trofei.

Grandpa Trapattoni is dreaming of seven Italian championships, a German Bundesliga, a Portuguese SuperLiga title, a European Cup, three UEFA cups, a Cup Winners' Cup, and a happy retirement in the sunshine.
Nonno Trapattoni sta sognando sette campionati italiani, una Bundesliga tedesca, un titolo della SuperLiga portoghese, una Coppa dei Campioni, tre Coppe Uefa, una Coppa delle Coppe e una tranquilla vita da pensionato in un luogo caldo.

Cerberus the dog enters the atrium.
Il cane Cerbero entra nell'atrio.

Learn to Speak Capello • 3

Cerberus looks around the atrium.
Cerbero dà un'occhiata in giro nell'atrio.

The precious trophies are very shiny. Grandpa Trapattoni snores.
I preziosi trofei brillano molto. Nonno Trapattoni russa.

Cerberus steals a trophy!
Cerbero ruba un trofeo!

Grandpa Trapattoni shakes his fist.
Nonno Trapattoni agita il pugno.

Fabio enters the atrium and turns on the television.
Fabio entra nell'atrio e accende il televisore.

'Bad dog!' shouts Grandpa Trapattoni.
'Cattivo!' urla nonno Trapattoni al cane.

A Euro 2008 qualifying match is on the television.
Alla tivù stanno trasmettendo una partita di qualificazione agli Europei del 2008.

A pink-faced, red-headed man watches the match. He has a magnificent umbrella.
Un uomo con il volto roseo e con i capelli rossi guarda la partita. Ha con sé un ombrello bellissimo.

Fabio shakes his head. Grandpa Trapattoni shakes his head. 'Bad dog!' mutters Grandpa Trapattoni.
Fabio scuote la testa. Nonno Trapattoni scuote la testa. 'Cattivo!' borbotta nonno Trapattoni.

Grammar: At Home

I sit, you sit, he sits, she sits, we sit, you sit (plural), they sit
Io sono seduto, tu sei seduto, lui è seduto, lei è seduta, noi siamo seduti, voi siete seduti, loro sono seduti

Example: I sit in the dugout.
Esempio: Sono seduto in panchina.

I dream, you dream, he dreams, she dreams, we dream, you dream, they dream
Io sogno, tu sogni, lui sogna, lei sogna, noi sogniamo, voi sognate, loro sognano

Example: I dream of having enough money to buy Chagall's painting *Bella with White Collar*.
Esempio: Sogno di avere denaro sufficiente per comprare 'Bella con il colletto bianco' di Chagall.

NB: In actual Italian usage, the personal pronoun can often be omitted when it is the subject of a verb. E.g. We dream = *sogniamo*.

Learn to Speak Capello • 7

Vocabulary: At Home

Umbrella
Un ombrello

Television set
Un televisore

Dog
Un cane

Statue
Una statua

Italian cup
La Coppa Italia

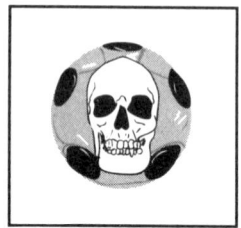

Group of death
Il gruppo della morte

Phrasebook: Press Conference Clichés

I'm looking forward to working more closely with the players.
Non vedo l'ora di avere un contatto più diretto con i giocatori.

Defence is the best form of attack.
La difesa è la miglior forma d'attacco.

Invest in skill, invest in hard work, invest in early cubist lithographs.
Investi nell'abilità, investi nel duro lavoro, investi in litografie protocubiste.

Gestures

Threat*
Minaccia
[Min-ATCH-ee-a]

*Perhaps to accompany the phrase: 'No Winalot for you tonight.'
'Niente Winalot per te stasera.'

What a bore
*Che palle**
[Kay PAL-ay]

*Literally 'what bollocks'. The metaphorical meaning extends to anything that is a burden or onerous to the speaker. Possible accompanying phrase: 'Watching England is like watching paint dry.'

> '*Guardare l'Inghilterra è una gran palla*' (literally 'Watching England is one big bollock').

Tactics Board
Capello's Legendary Teams No.1: The Private Art Collection

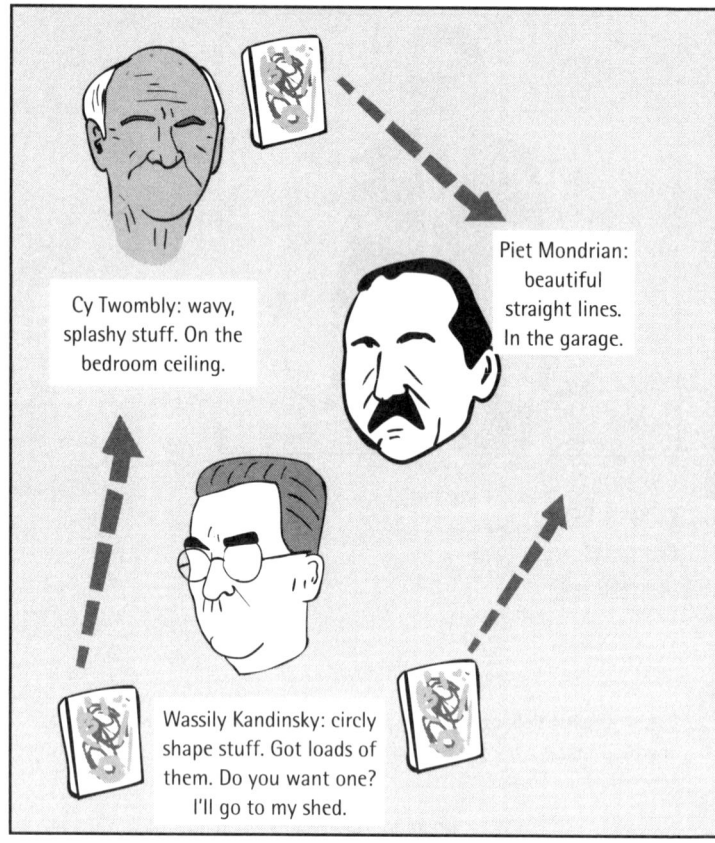

History

*James Richardson Spensley
Invented Italian Football*

Born in north London, this archetypal Edwardian sporting gent-doctor-foreign correspondent-polymath also had a sideline in scouting – of the Baden Powell variety. Organized the first game of football in Italy at Genoa in 1897 at what was then a cricket and athletics club. Died in WWI while tending enemy wounded. A quiet life.

History

Italy's Football Greats

William Garbutt
The original 'Il Mister'

Became manager of Genoa in 1912. Successfully introduced English-style organization and fitness-training methods (once upon a time they were seen as progressive). Also managed Roma and Napoli. So far the only man from Stockport to have won three Italian league titles.

Module Two
Modulo Due

In the Workplace
Al Lavoro

The Football Association is having a meeting with Steve McClaren.

La Football Association è in riunione con Steve McClaren.

'Hello, Steve McClaren,' says the FA, smiling in a strange way.

'Salve, McClaren,' dice la FA, sorridendo in modo strano.

'They look like nice, friendly old men,' thinks Steve McClaren.

'Sembrano dei vecchietti simpatici,' pensa Steve McClaren.

Steve McClaren sees a large knife.
Steve McClaren vede un grande coltello.

'Look over there – it's an umbrella shop!' says the FA.
'Guarda là – un negozio di ombrelli!' dice la FA.

Steve McClaren loves umbrellas. He turns around to look at them. He no longer sees the large knife.
Steve McClaren va pazzo per gli ombrelli. Si gira per guardarli. Non vede più il grande coltello.

'Arrrgh . . . a few years of radio punditry, then,' thinks Steve McClaren.
'Aaaah . . . qualche anno di opinionismo alla radio, dunque,' pensa Steve McClaren.

Learn to Speak Capello • 19

The FA is in crisis. The FA calls an urgent crisis meeting.
La FA è in crisi. La FA convoca una riunione urgentissima.

The urgent crisis meeting lasts for several months. The FA decides to buy a telephone.
La riunione urgentissima dura qualche mese. La FA decide di comprare un telefono.

Should the FA call an Italian man with glasses who has won everything in the game? Or Sam Allardyce, who once got to the final of the Carling Cup?
Dovrebbe forse chiamare quel signore italiano occhialuto che ha già vinto tutto? Oppure Sam Allardyce, che una volta è arrivato alla finale della Carling Cup?

At Fabio's house, Uncle Silvio has arrived. 'Are you well, Uncle Silvio?' asks Fabio.
A casa di Fabio è arrivato lo zio Silvio. 'Stai bene, zio Silvio?' chiede Fabio.

'Yes. I've just had to resign the chairmanship of AC Milan again!' laughs Uncle Silvio. They all laugh.
'Si. Mi sono appena dovuto ridimettere dalla presidenza del Milan!' ride zio Silvio. Ridono tutti.

Cerberus the dog gives a Guinness bottle to Grandpa Trap. There is a message inside. 'Good dog,' says Grandpa Trap.
Il cane Cerbero dà una bottiglia di Guinness a nonno Trapattoni. Dentro c'è un messaggio. 'Bravo!' dice nonno Trapattoni al cane.

The FA telephones Fabio about a job. The FA likes to play 'hardball'. 'Will you manage England for £4 million a year?' asks the FA.

La FA chiama Fabio per un lavoro. La FA gioca sempre duro. 'Vuoi allenare l'Inghilterra per 4 milioni di sterline all'anno?' chiede la FA.

Fabio accidentally drops a framed Dali sketch.

Fabio lascia cadere accidentalmente un disegno incorniciato di Dalì.

The FA is worried by the frightening noise. '£6 million?'

La FA si spaventa per il gran fracasso. '6 milioni?'

'OK,' laughs Fabio and slaps Grandpa Trapattoni on the back.

'OK,' ride Fabio e dà una pacca sulla schiena a nonno Trapattoni.

Grammar: In the Workplace

I will go, you will go, he will go, she will go, we will go, you will go, they will go
Io andrò, tu andrai, lui andrà, lei andrà, noi andremo, voi andrete, loro andranno

Example: I will go abroad for a couple of years to coach a football team.
Esempio: Andrò all'estero per un paio d'anni per allenare una squadra di calcio.

I hope, you hope, he hopes, she hopes, we hope, you hope, they hope
Io spero, tu speri, lui spera, lei spera, noi speriamo, voi sperate, loro sperano

Example: I hope my friends feed the dog while I'm gone.
Esempio: Spero che i miei amici diano da mangiare al cane mentre sono via.

Learn to Speak Capello • 23

Vocabulary: In the Workplace

Large Knife
Un grande coltello

Umbrella shop
Un negozio di ombrelli

Kind old man
Un vecchietto gentile

Telephone
Un telefono

Contract
Un contratto

Bottle of Guinness
Una bottiglia di Guinness

Phrasebook: Press Conference Clichés

I have a great relationship with Silvio Berlusconi.
Con Silvio Berlusconi ho un ottimo rapporto.

I have a great relationship with David Beckham.
Con David Beckham ho un ottimo rapporto.

I have a great relationship with the tabloid press.
Con i tabloid ho un ottimo rapporto.

Gestures

Contentment/Happiness
Contentezza
[Con-ten-TETZ-a]

*Perhaps to accompany the phrase: 'I am so happy to be going to sunny England.'

Sono proprio contento di andare in Inghilterra. Almeno li fa caldo.

History

Inter Milan coach in the 1960s, Herrera developed the highly defensive 'catenaccio' system. Under his guidance '1-0' took on a new beauty. His most famous quote is, 'He who doesn't give it all, gives nothing.' (Perhaps referring to parsimonious relatives during the Christmas season.)

History

Italy's Football Greats

Enzo Bearzot
An Italian Ron Greenwood

Italy's coach from 1977 to 1986. Led his country to World Cup glory in 1982, during which they beat everyone's favourite team, Brazil. Was always getting namechecked by Denis Law on ITV football shows.

Games: 'Catenaccio'

Catenaccio is sometimes misunderstood as being a defensive and negative tactic, when really it is filled with grace, beauty, profound philosophical truth and religious awe. Test your knowledge of this sacred art below:

Question 1: You are 1-0 up after five minutes. Do you:
    a) Go for it
    b) Shut up shop and get out the armchair

Question 2: You need a goal. Do you:
    a) Go for all-out attack
    b) Fall over in the opposition's penalty area

Question 3: You see referees as:
    a) Annoyances
    b) Gentlemen who have their own needs and wants

Question 4: At home you relax by watching:
    a) Goal highlight videos
    b) Tackle highlight videos

If you answered **mostly 'a'** – you are not a successful coach and you don't know anything about football.

If you answered **mostly 'b'** – you see football as a beautiful game and you play it the right way: with fear and caution.

Tactics Board
Bearzot's Legendary Team: Italy at Euro 1980

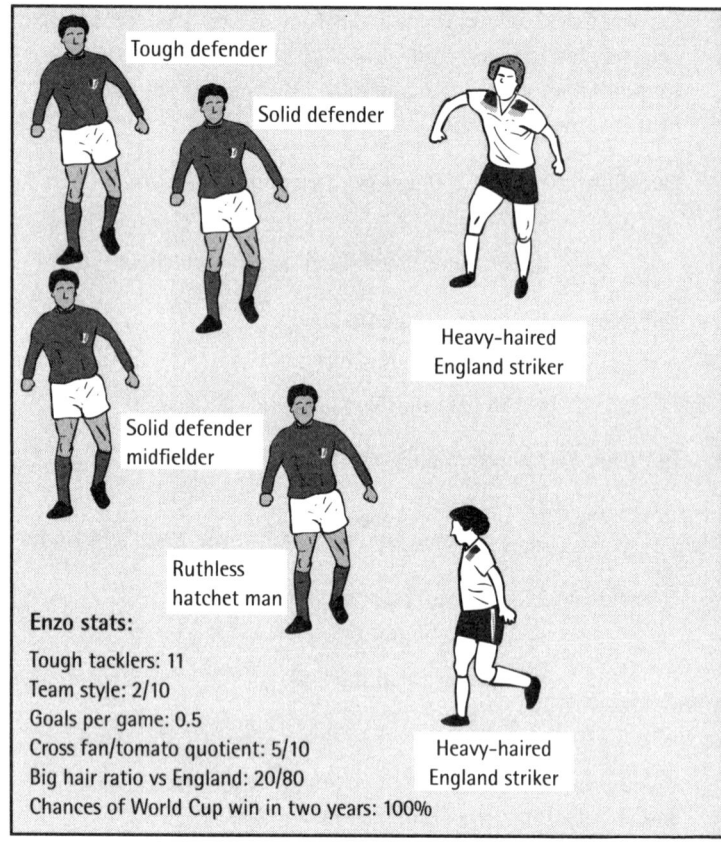

Slow, thin, gargantuan-haired England right back

Speedy winger

fig.1

fig.2

'The England team all have massive hair, but their right back, Phil Neal, has the heaviest hair in Europe, which will slow him up. We must exploit this.'

Learn to Speak Capello • 31

Module Three
Modulo Tre

Travelling Abroad
Viaggiare All'Estero

Fabio gets on a plane to London. 'Are you coming?' he asks Grandpa Trapattoni.

Fabio prende l'aereo per Londra. 'Vieni anche tu?' chiede a nonno Trapattoni.

'No, I've been offered a job in Ireland,' says Grandpa Trapattoni.

'No, mi hanno offerto un lavoro in Irlanda,' risponde nonno Trapattoni.

Grandpa Trapattoni shows Fabio the message from the bottle. The note says: 'Please help! – Love the FAI x.'

Nonno Trapattoni mostra a Fabio il messaggio della bottiglia. Il biglietto dice: 'Aiuto! Un affettuoso abbraccio, la FA Irlandese x.'

On the plane, Fabio is thinking about English football. Fabio once had Gullit and Van Basten in his team. Now he will have Dean Ashton and Peter Crouch.

Sull'aereo, Fabio pensa al calcio inglese. Una volta Fabio aveva in squadra Gullit e Van Basten. Ora potrà contare su Dean Ashton e Peter Crouch.

Fabio gets a strange buzzing in his head.
Fabio sente uno strano ronzio in testa.

Fabio wants the buzzing to go away, but when he closes his eyes all he can see is Peter Crouch doing a funny dance. Like a robot.
Fabio vorrebbe che il ronzio cessasse, ma quando chiude gli occhi vede solo Peter Crouch che sta ballando una strana danza. Come un robot.

At Heathrow Airport the press is waiting.
All'aeroporto di Heathrow la stampa sta aspettando.

'Do you think England can win the next World Cup?' asks the press. Fabio laughs and pretends not to understand.
'Credi che l'Inghilterra potrà vincere i prossimi Mondiali?' chiede. Fabio ride e fa finta di non capire.

The press hopes Fabio will be very successful, or better still rubbish so it can crucify him after an initial honeymoon period.
La stampa sarà contenta se Fabio avrà molto successo, ma sarà ancora più contenta se fallirà clamorosamente, così potrà crocifiggerlo dopo l'idillio iniziale.

The FA holds a press conference. The FA hopes no one will ask why they didn't all resign.
La FA tiene una conferenza stampa. Quelli della FA sperano che nessuno chieda loro perché non si siano tutti dimessi.

Fabio is wondering whether to tell everyone his no.1 tactical secret – the one about the two holding midfield players.
Fabio si sta chiedendo se non sia il caso di rivelare a tutti quanti il suo segreto tattico numero 1 – quello dei due mediani d'interdizione.

In the end, Fabio just smiles and pretends not to understand.
Alla fine Fabio si limita a sorridere e finge di non capire.

Grandpa Trapattoni has travelled all the way around Ireland. He is looking for the Football Association of Ireland.

Nonno Trapattoni ha fatto il giro di tutta l'Irlanda. Sta cercando la FA Irlandese.

Grandpa Trapattoni finds the FAI on a fishing boat in Dublin Bay. The boat has a leak and is listing to one side.

Nonno Trapattoni trova la FA Irlandese su un peschereccio nella baia di Dublino. La barca fa acqua e pende tutta da un lato.

Grandpa Trapattoni sighs, unpacks his suitcase and helpfully plugs the leak with his spare Austrian championship trophy.

Nonno Trapattoni sospira, disfa la valigia e premurosamente tappa la falla con il trofeo di scorta vinto nel campionato austriaco.

Grammar: Travelling Abroad

I am wondering, you are wondering, he is wondering, she is wondering, we are wondering, you are wondering, they are wondering.

Io mi sto chiedendo, tu ti stai chiedendo, lui si sta chiedendo, lei si sta chiedendo, noi ci stiamo chiedendo, voi vi state chiedendo, loro si stanno chiedendo.

Example: I am wondering whether to tell them my secret tactic.

Esempio: Mi sto chiedendo se non sia il caso di rivelar loro la mia tattica segreta.

I am, you are, he is, she is, we are, you are, they are.

Io sono, tu sei, lui è, lei è, noi siamo, voi siete, loro sono.

Example: They are very generous.

Esempio: Loro sono molto generosi.

Learn to Speak Capello • 39

Vocabulary: Travelling Abroad

Aeroplane
Un aereo

Complimentary peanuts
Arachidi omaggio

Travel pass
Un abbonamento

Top-secret journal
Un taccuino top-secret

Fishing boat
Un peschereccio

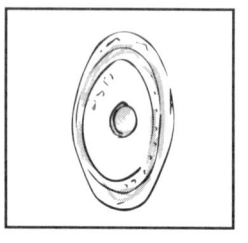

Austrian Championship trophy
Un trofeo del campionato austriaco

Phrasebook: Press Conference Clichés

It is an honour to be managing this team.
È un onore allenare questa squadra.

I'm sure I can get the best out of Wayne Rooney.
Sono certo di poter tirare fuori il meglio da Wayne Rooney.

England are well regarded in football circles.
L'Inghilterra gode di grande rispetto nell'ambiente calcistico.

Learn to Speak Capello

Gestures

Hello!
Ciao!*
[TchOW!]

---

*'Hello England, you look pale and a bit flabby and rather clueless about zonal marking.'

'Ciao Inghilterra, mi sembrate un tantino palliducci, un po' flosci e scarsetti in fatto di marcatura a zona.'

Gestures

Don't worry about it

Non ti preoccupare

[Non tee pray-ok-oo-PAR-ay]

Sample usage: 'Everyone should just chill out about World Cup qualification.'

'Dovreste prendervela di meno per la qualificazione ai Mondiali.'

History

Italy's Football Greats

Dino Zoff
Nearly won Euro 2000

Didn't get a long stint at managing Italy thanks to a bust-up with Silvio Berlusconi. He was twenty seconds away from winning Euro 2000 with Italy and was probably already mulling over the tracklist for the celebration party (some mid-period Beatles and a bit of Santana, perhaps) when France equalized in injury time.

Italy's Football Greats

Arrigo Sacchi
Tried to destroy catenaccio

Sacchi's great Milan side of the late 1980s/early 90s displayed that most un-Italian of attributes, an attacking 4-4-2 system. His innovative non-defensive ideas didn't catch on and when he left he was replaced by, erm, Fabio Capello. His brief reign as Italy manager coincided with their tag of lovable underdogs. And contrary to popular opinion he is not Greta Scacchi's dad.

Games: Comparisons

Here are some of the recent England managers. What were they like in relation to Fabio?

Steve McClaren loves umbrellas more than Fabio
Steve McClaren ama gli ombrelli più di Fabio

Sven Goran Eriksson is more highly sexed than Fabio
Sven Goran Eriksson è più arrapato di Fabio

Kevin Keegan's teams have more defensive frailties than those of Fabio
Le squadre di Kevin Keegan hanno più debolezze difensive di quelle di Fabio

Fabio is less spiritual than Glenn Hoddle
Fabio è meno spirituale di Glenn Hoddle

Fabio is less entrepreneurially minded than Terry Venables
Fabio è meno imprenditoriale di Terry Venables

Fabio is less Geordie than Bobby Robson
Fabio è meno Geordie di Bobby Robson

Fabio is completely different to Graham Taylor
Fabio è completamente diverso da Graham Taylor

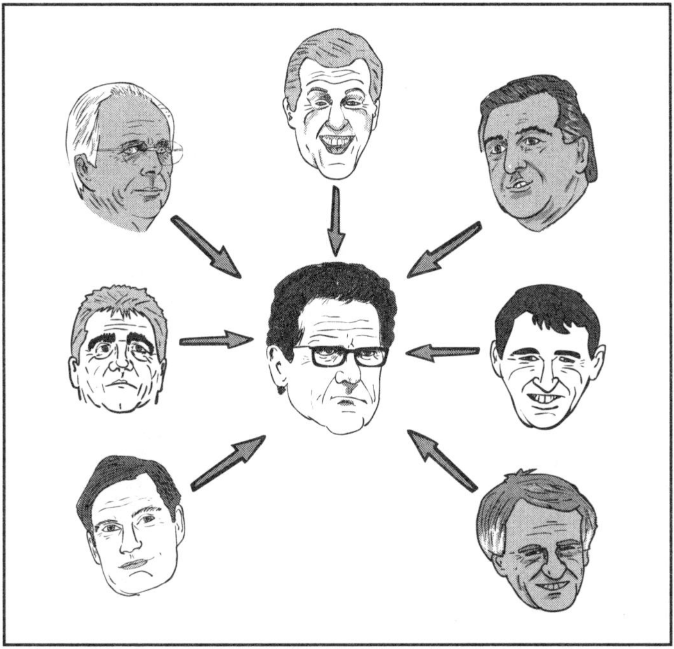

Tactics Board
Zoff's Legendary Team: Italy at Euro 2000

Some big hard bloke

Big tough defender

Big tough midfielder

The Zoffmeister

Got a collection of Alice bands

Got a nice Alice band

Borrowed a nice Alice band

Had quite a few Alice bands but left them in the hotel room and borrowed one from the other bloke. At first he thought the other bloke had stolen his Alice bands, but they'd got a different label. He could have switched the labels, of course, but it's unlikely, as they were about to play an important Euro 2000 match. He'll double check when he gets back to the hotel.

48 • Learn to Speak Capello

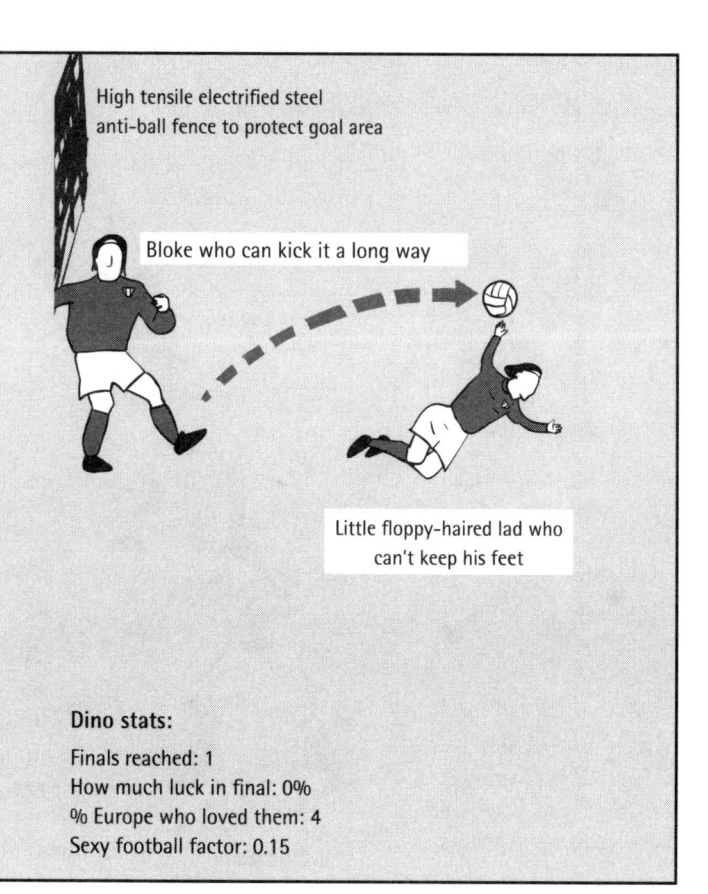

High tensile electrified steel anti-ball fence to protect goal area

Bloke who can kick it a long way

Little floppy-haired lad who can't keep his feet

Dino stats:

Finals reached: 1
How much luck in final: 0%
% Europe who loved them: 4
Sexy football factor: 0.15

Learn to Speak Capello • 49

Tactics Board
Trapattoni's Legendary Teams No.1: Italy at Euro 2004

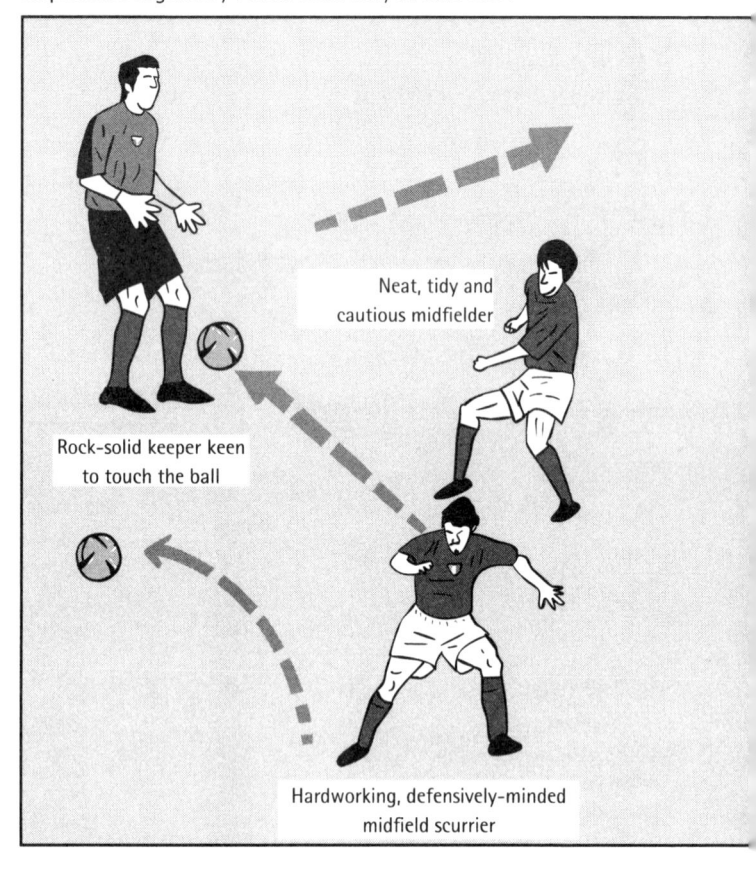

Neat, tidy and cautious midfielder

Rock-solid keeper keen to touch the ball

Hardworking, defensively-minded midfield scurrier

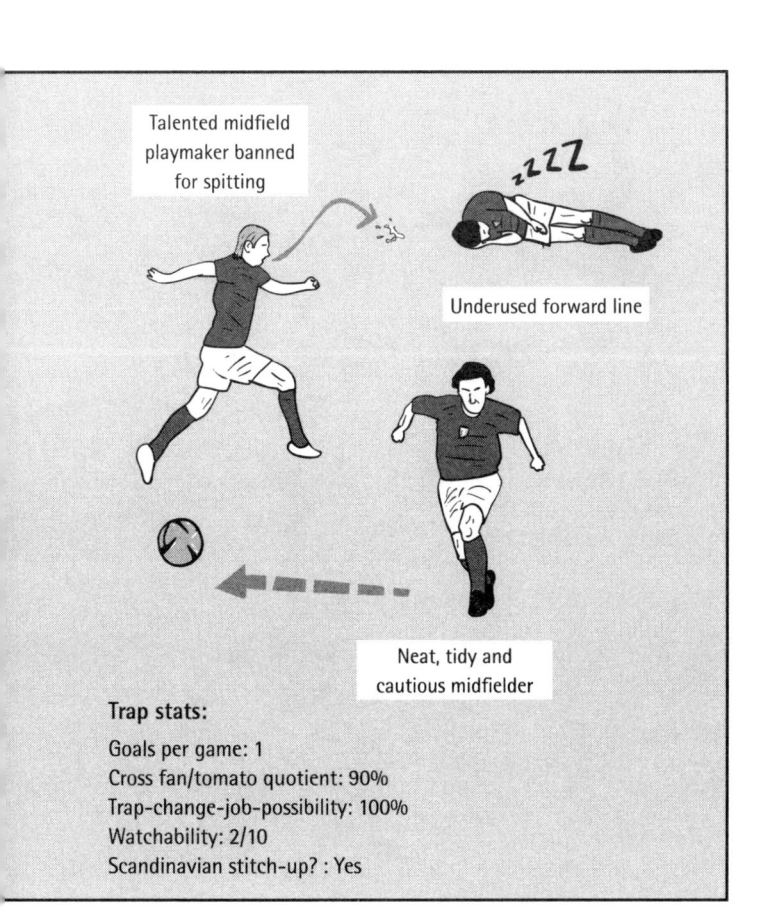

Talented midfield playmaker banned for spitting

Underused forward line

Neat, tidy and cautious midfielder

Trap stats:

Goals per game: 1
Cross fan/tomato quotient: 90%
Trap-change-job-possibility: 100%
Watchability: 2/10
Scandinavian stitch-up? : Yes

Learn to Speak Capello • 51

Tactics Board
Trapattoni's Legendary Teams No.2: Ireland

Defender who sometimes looks good on the telly when he's playing for Manchester United

Keeper best player in team. And needs to be to keep scores respectable

Hardworking defensive clogger

52 • Learn to Speak Capello

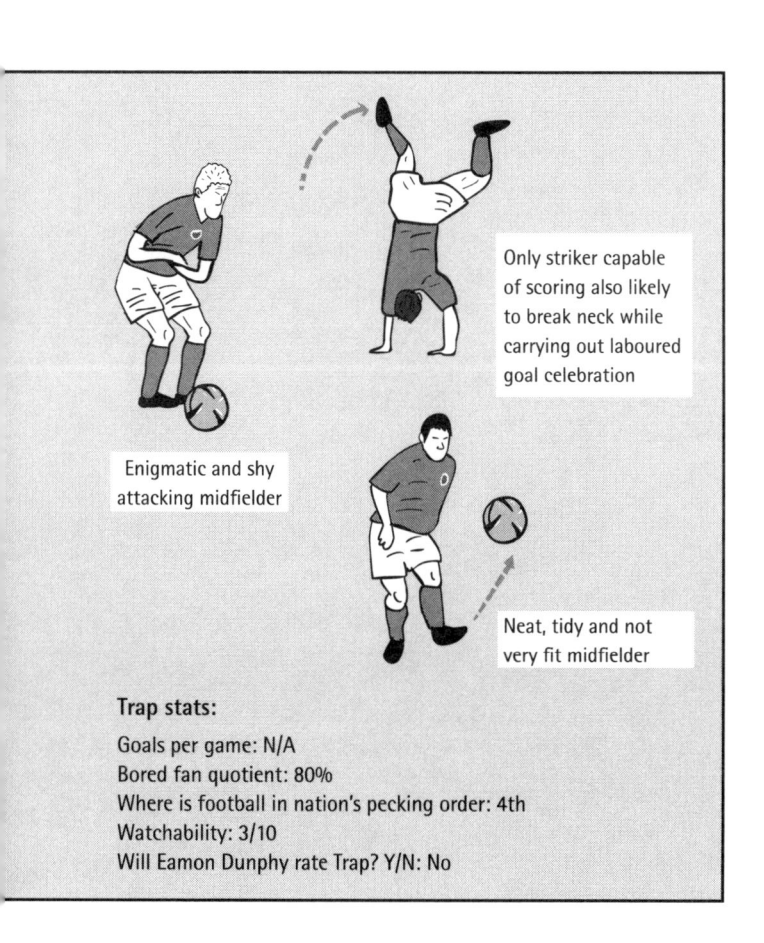

Only striker capable of scoring also likely to break neck while carrying out laboured goal celebration

Enigmatic and shy attacking midfielder

Neat, tidy and not very fit midfielder

Trap stats:

Goals per game: N/A
Bored fan quotient: 80%
Where is football in nation's pecking order: 4th
Watchability: 3/10
Will Eamon Dunphy rate Trap? Y/N: No

Module Four
Modulo Quattro

Sport and Pastimes
Sport e Tempo Libero

Fabio is about to meet the England players at Bisham Abbey, with his interpreter.

Fabio sta per incontrare i giocatori inglesi a Bisham Abbey, con il suo interprete.

'These are beautiful grounds. And there are nice fountains and statues here,' says Fabio. 'Is that a Henry Moore?'

'Questo è un parco veramente magnifico. E anche le fontane e le statue sono belle,' dice Fabio. 'È forse una Henry Moore, quella?'

'No,' says the interpreter. 'That is John Terry.'

'No,' dice l'interprete. 'Quello è John Terry.'

At a meeting the players listen. The players listen to Fabio.
I giocatori sono presenti ad una riunione. I giocatori stanno ascoltando Fabio.

Fabio tells them his no.1 tactical secret. Gareth Barry and Owen Hargreaves look pleased.
Fabio gli rivela il suo segreto tattico numero 1. Gareth Barry e Owen Hargreaves sembrano soddisfatti.

The other midfield players look cross. 'That's a daft idea,' they say.
Gli altri centrocampisti sembrano seccati. 'Che idea cretina,' dicono.

Fabio shouts. The midfield players now know who is in charge.
Fabio urla. Ora i centrocampisti capiscono chi è che comanda.

Fabio holds his first training session. Fabio is surprised by the quality of the players. Nobody knows if the surprise is a pleasant one.

Fabio tiene il suo primo allenamento. Fabio è sorpreso dalla qualità dei giocatori. Non è chiaro se la sorpresa sia piacevole.

Fabio approaches Michael Owen with a friendly smile.

Fabio si avvicina a Michael Owen con un sorriso amichevole.

Fabio locks Michael Owen in a trunk and explains to Wayne Rooney that he may be spending more time alone from now on.

Fabio chiude Michael Owen in un baule e spiega a Wayne Rooney che da ora innanzi dovrà rassegnarsi ad essere un po' più solo.

Fabio goes for a meal with the players. Fabio looks confused.
Fabio va a mangiar fuori con i giocatori. Fabio sembra perplesso.

'You have the wrong proportions of protein and carbohydrates,' says Fabio. The players look confused.
'Le proporzioni di proteine e di carboidrati che assumete sono sbagliate,' dice Fabio. I giocatori lo guardano perplessi.

Fabio puts more pasta on Wayne Rooney's plate. 'Rooney must not get thin!' says Fabio.
Fabio aggiunge dell'altra pasta nel piatto di Wayne Rooney. 'Rooney non deve dimagrire!' dice Fabio.

The players laugh and drink some beer.
I giocatori ridono e bevono della birra.

The players invite Fabio to a party at Chinawhite's disco.
I giocatori invitano Fabio a una festa alla Chinawhite's disco.

Fabio telephones Grandpa Trapattoni. 'These players are crazy!' says Fabio.
Fabio telefona a nonno Trapattoni. 'Ma questi giocatori sono proprio matti!' dice Fabio.

'I can't talk now,' says Grandpa Trapattoni. 'I am out on the town with my new best friend, Roy Keane.'
'Non posso parlare adesso,' dice nonno Trapattoni. 'Sto facendo baldoria con il mio nuovo grande amico, Roy Keane.'

Grammar: Sport and Pastimes

I disapprove, you disapprove, he disapproves, she disapproves, we disapprove, you disapprove, they disapprove

Io disapprovo, tu disapprovi, lui disapprova, lei disapprova, noi disapproviamo, voi disapprovate, loro disapprovano

Example: I disapprove of large quantities of chips with each meal.

Esempio: Disapprovo il fatto che si mangino grandi quantità di patatine fritte ad ogni pasto.

I rehydrate myself, you rehydrate yourself, he rehydrates himself, she rehydrates herself, we rehydrate ourselves, you rehydrate yourselves, they rehydrate themselves.

Io mi reidrato, tu ti reidrati, lui si reidrata, lei si reidrata, noi ci reidratiamo, voi vi reidratate, loro si reidratano.

Example: The players must rehydrate between games.

Esempio: I giocatori devono reidratarsi tra una partita e l'altra.

Learn to Speak Capello • 61

Vocabulary: Sport and Pastimes

Smart coaching facility
Un impianto di allenamento di lusso

Sports technique equipment
Attrezzi per l'apprendimento della tecnica sportiva

Statue
Una statua

Balanced nutrition
Una alimentazione equilibrata

Sports drink
Una bevanda energetica

Robotic dancing
Danza robotica

Phrasebook: Press Conference Clichés

England has several world-class players.
L'Inghilterra ha parecchi fuoriclasse.

We're all singing from the same hymn sheet.
Siamo una squadra unita. (Literally: 'We are a united team.')

Rooney just has a lot of relaxed fast-twitch muscle fibre.
È solo che Rooney ha un sacco di fibre muscolari a contrazione rapida.

Gestures

'Bottled-up anger'
Collera interna
[Koll-air-a in-TER-na]

Perhaps to accompany the phrase: 'I can't believe that no one in this squad can do more than twelve keepie-uppies.'

'Non posso credere che nessuno in questa squadra riesca a fare più di dodici palleggi per volta.'

Gestures

I have eaten well
Ho mangiato bene
[Oh man-gee-AH-toe ben-ay]

Perhaps to accompany the phrase: 'Please boss, no more pasta!'
'*Per favore mister, basta pasta!*'

History

Italy's Football Greats

Marcello Lippi
World Cup winner

After a successful stint at Juventus, Lippi had just two years as Italy's coach, during which they won the World Cup. Lippi then (very sensibly) resigned to spend more time with his medals and trophies... Before accepting the job again after Euro 2008.

History

Italy's Football Greats

Carlo Ancelotti
Has he always been at Milan?

Still only in his forties, Ancelotti has already won a Scudetto and two Champions League trophies with Milan. One day there he was playing in the 1994 final, the next minute he's in a suit being all grown up. Where does the time go? Of course, he did age ten years during the second half of the 2005 Champions League final against Liverpool.

Games: Fabio's Kit Bag

Fabio likes clothes. Help him choose the right outfit for each occasion.

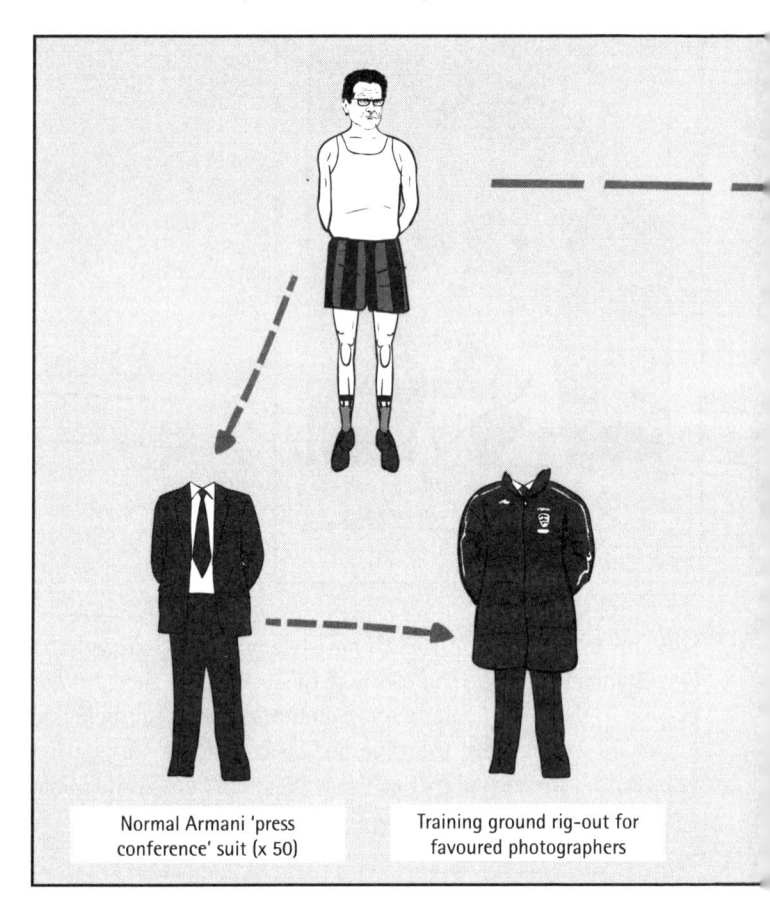

Normal Armani 'press conference' suit (x 50)

Training ground rig-out for favoured photographers

68 • Learn to Speak Capello

Tweeds for when meeting royalty, aristocracy and rural FA members

Lucky motivational gold-leaf suit-and-tie combo for half-time talk when team is behind

Pearly King outfit for when scouting incognito at London clubs

Something casual for going for a drink with the players or when veteran right-sided midfielders have a book launch

Learn to Speak Capello • 69

Module Five
Modulo Cinque

Match Day
Il Giorno Della Partita

It's the start of the World Cup qualification campaign.
È l'inizio della campagna di qualificazione ai Mondiali.

'Defence is the best form of attack,' says Fabio. Fabio winks at Gareth Barry and Owen Hargreaves.
'La difesa è la miglior forma di attacco,' dice Fabio. Fabio strizza l'occhio a Gareth Barry e a Owen Hargreaves.

The other midfielders scowl at Gareth Barry and Owen Hargreaves.
Gli altri centrocampisti guardano Barry e Hargreaves di brutto.

Fabio shouts at the other midfield players.
Fabio urla agli altri centrocampisti.

The FA comes to visit Fabio.
La FA va a far visita a Fabio.

The FA wants reassurances from Fabio that England will definitely win the World Cup. 'After all,' they say, 'you did such a great job with Italy in 2006, Mr Lippi!'
La FA vuole delle garanzie da parte di Fabio che l'Inghilterra vincerà la Coppa del Mondo. 'In fin dei conti,' dice, 'lei ha fatto un ottimo lavoro con l'Italia nel 2006, signor Lippi.'

Fabio suddenly feels very tired.
Fabio si sente improvvisamente molto stanco.

Fabio telephones Grandpa Trapattoni.
Fabio telefona a nonno Trapattoni.

'Don't you miss Italy?' Fabio asks Grandpa Trapattoni.
'Non hai nostalgia dell'Italia?' Fabio chiede a nonno Trapattoni.

'Can't talk,' says Grandpa Trapattoni. 'I'm in a three-round bare-fist boxing match against Dunphy and Giles, the RTE football pundits.'
'Non posso parlare adesso,' dice nonno Trapattoni. 'Sono impegnato in un incontro di pugilato a mani nude in tre round contro Dunphy e Giles, i moviolisti della televisione irlandese.'

Fabio is unhappy, but he cheers up when he sees a handsome stone figure in the corner of the room.

Fabio si sente un po' giù, ma si tira su quando vede una bella figura di pietra nell'angolo della stanza.

'A lovely piece,' says Fabio. 'Such graceful lines, such a sense of stillness, unmoving, frozen in time. Is it a Giacometti?'

'È un pezzo bellissimo,' dice Fabio. 'Ha delle linee così eleganti, una tale fissità, è così immobile, fermo nel tempo. È forse un Giacometti?'

'No, that's John Terry,' says Rio Ferdinand.

'No, è John Terry,' dice Rio Ferdinand.

Learn to Speak Capello • 75

Fabio looks at the England players singing the national anthem.

Fabio guarda i giocatori inglesi cantare l'inno nazionale.

Fabio's head is buzzing again. Fabio wants the buzzing to go away.

Fabio sente di nuovo quel ronzio in testa. Fabio vorrebbe che il ronzio cessasse.

The referee blows his whistle and the game begins.

L'arbitro fischia e la partita inizia.

Grammar: Match Day

I run, you run, he runs, she runs, we run, you run, they run

Io corro, tu corri, lui corre, lei corre, noi corriamo, voi correte, loro corrono

Example: The players run around for ninety minutes like headless chickens.

Esempio: I giocatori corrono per novanta minuti come un branco di imbecilli (literally 'like a bunch of idiots').

I need, you need, he needs, she needs, we need, you need, they need

Io ho bisogno, tu hai bisogno, lui ha bisogno, lei ha bisogno, noi abbiamo bisogno, voi avete bisogno, loro hanno bisogno

Example: They need to work on some basic ball skills.

Esempio: Hanno bisogno di esercitarsi in alcune tecniche base di palleggio.

Learn to Speak Capello • 77

Vocabulary: Match Day

To deal with pressure
Far fronte allo stress

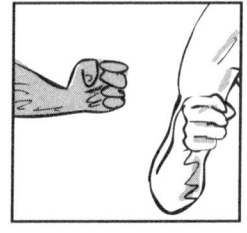

Bare-knuckle boxing
Pugilato a mani nude

Holding midfielders
Mediani d'interdizione

Tired
Stanco

World Cup
La Coppa del Mondo

Dodgy refs
Arbitri discutibili

Phrasebook: Press Conference Clichés

On the contrary, I think the two holding midfield players worked brilliantly.
Al contrario, credo che il sistema dei due mediani d'interdizione abbia funzionato benissimo.

There are no easy games in international football.
Non esistono partite facili nel calcio internazionale.

I did not see the incident you are talking about.
Non ho visto l'episodio di cui parla.

Gestures

Excellent
Eccellente!
[Etch-a-LENT-ay]

Possible use: 'Gareth Barry has an instinctive understanding of the two holding midfielders theory.'
Gareth Barry ha una predisposizione innata per il sistema dei due mediani d'interdizione.

Gestures

Cheers!
Salute!
[Sal-OOT-ay]

Perhaps to accompany the phrase: 'Rejoice! England have done OK against modest opposition.'
'Evviva! L'Inghilterra s'è comportata benino contro un avversario mediocre.'

History

Italy's Football Greats

Fabio Capello
Sensible football mastermind

Happily minding his own business in retirement when the FA came a-calling. Capello has won a shedload of Serie A titles, the Champions League in 1994 and was capped over thirty times for Italy as a player. He even won La Liga with Real Madrid, after which he was immediately sacked. No wonder he looks angry.

History

Italy's Football Greats

Giovanni Trapattoni
Trophy machine

Won seven league titles with Juventus from the mid 1970s and lots of other trophies elsewhere. Coached Italy in their ill-fated 2002 World Cup and Euro 2004 attempts. For all that silverware, we still remember him for getting mad at FIFA conspiracies when South Korea knocked out Italy in 2002. The Italian Jack Charlton?

Tactics Board
Capello's Legendary Teams No.2: AC Milan 1990-94

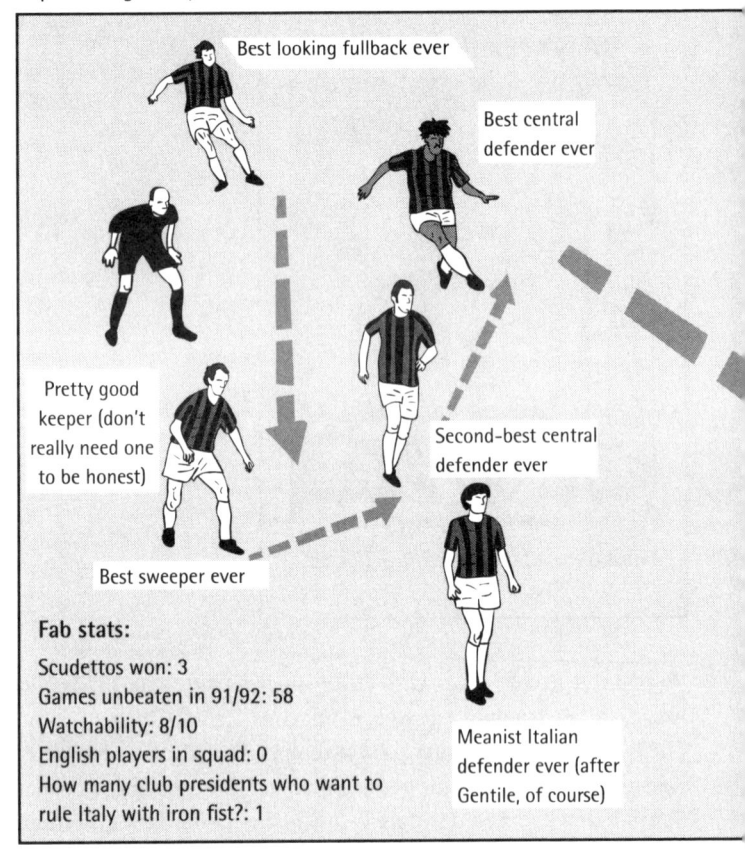

Best looking fullback ever

Best central defender ever

Pretty good keeper (don't really need one to be honest)

Second-best central defender ever

Best sweeper ever

Fab stats:

Scudettos won: 3
Games unbeaten in 91/92: 58
Watchability: 8/10
English players in squad: 0
How many club presidents who want to rule Italy with iron fist?: 1

Meanist Italian defender ever (after Gentile, of course)

84 • Learn to Speak Capello

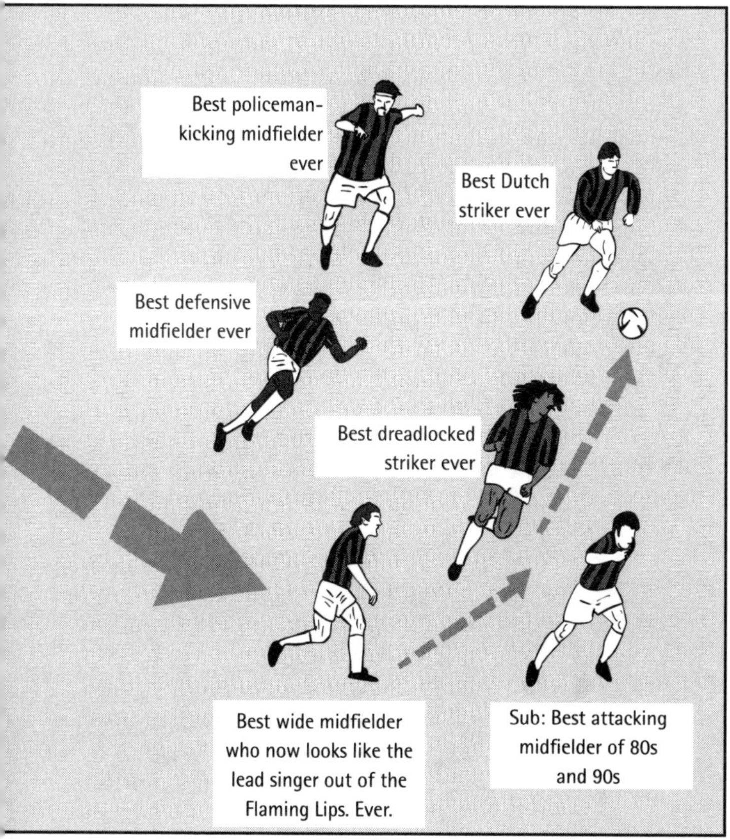
Best policeman-kicking midfielder ever
Best Dutch striker ever
Best defensive midfielder ever
Best dreadlocked striker ever
Best wide midfielder who now looks like the lead singer out of the Flaming Lips. Ever.
Sub: Best attacking midfielder of 80s and 90s

Tactics Board
Capello's Legendary Teams No.3: England

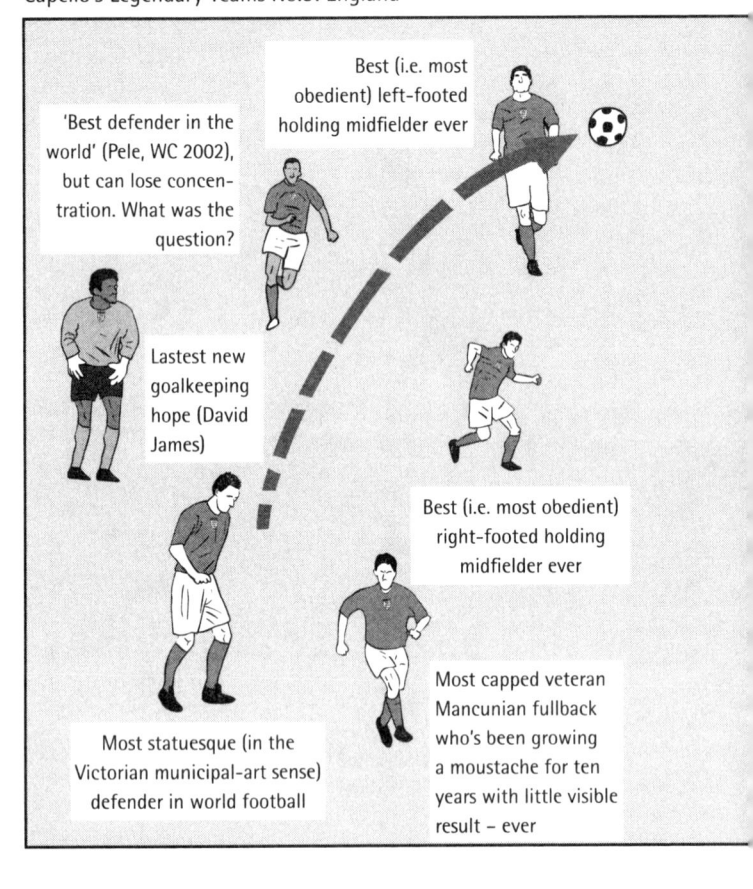

'Best defender in the world' (Pele, WC 2002), but can lose concentration. What was the question?

Best (i.e. most obedient) left-footed holding midfielder ever

Lastest new goalkeeping hope (David James)

Best (i.e. most obedient) right-footed holding midfielder ever

Most statuesque (in the Victorian municipal-art sense) defender in world football

Most capped veteran Mancunian fullback who's been growing a moustache for ten years with little visible result – ever

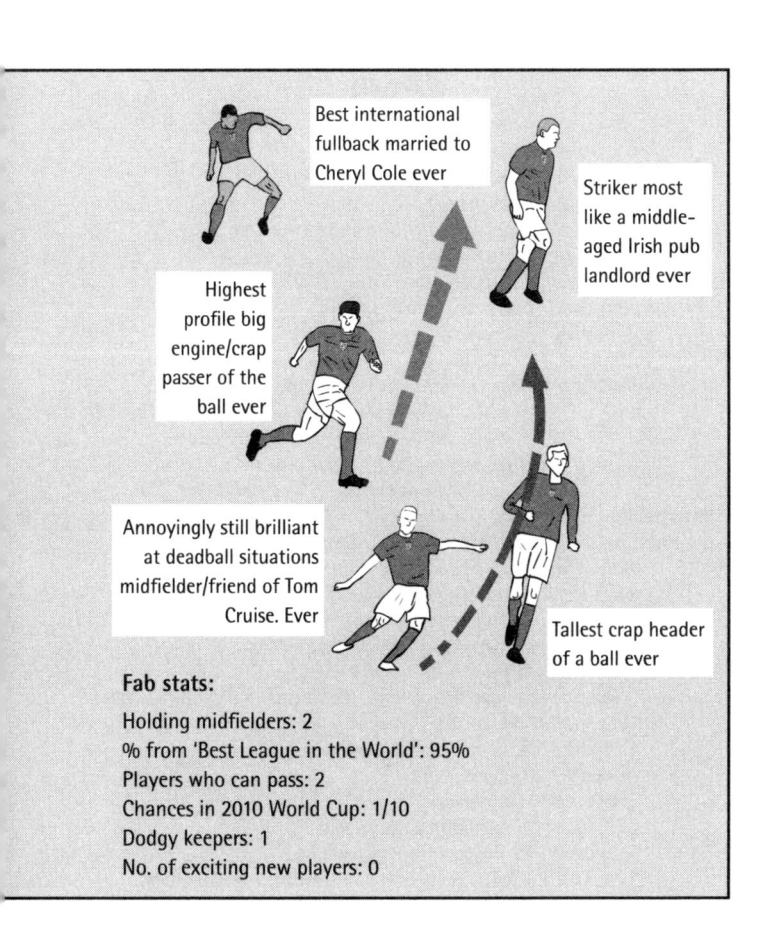

Best international fullback married to Cheryl Cole ever

Striker most like a middle-aged Irish pub landlord ever

Highest profile big engine/crap passer of the ball ever

Annoyingly still brilliant at deadball situations midfielder/friend of Tom Cruise. Ever

Tallest crap header of a ball ever

Fab stats:

Holding midfielders: 2
% from 'Best League in the World': 95%
Players who can pass: 2
Chances in 2010 World Cup: 1/10
Dodgy keepers: 1
No. of exciting new players: 0

Glossary

attack	*l'attacco (n.); attaccare (vb)*
attacker	*l'attaccante (n.)*
ball	*il pallone (n.)*
bench	*la panchina (n.); in panchina* = on the bench
booking	*l'ammonizione (n.);* to book = *ammonire (vb)*
captain	*il capitano (n.)*
centre back	*il terzino centrale (n.)*
chairman	*il presidente (n.)*
champion	*il campione (n.)*
championship	*il campionato (n.);* also *lo scudetto*, 'the shield'. From the 1923–24 season, the winners of the Italian championship were allowed to sew the colours of the national flag in a shield on their vests for the following season.
championship table	*la classifica (n.)*
chest (the ball)	*controllare di petto (la palla) (vb)*
corner flag	*la bandierina d'angolo (n.)*
corner kick	*calcio d'angolo (n.)*, also simply *un corner; battere un calcio d'angolo* = to take a corner
cross	*il cross (n); il traversone (n.);* to cross the ball = *fare un cross*
crossbar	*la traversa (n.);* to hit the crossbar = *prendere la traversa (vb);* to hit the woodwork = *prendere il legno (vb)*
defeat	*la sconfitta (n.); battere (vb)*
defender	*il difensore (n.)*
defence	*la difesa (n.)*
dive	*tuffarsi (also buttarsi) (vb)*
draw	*il pareggio (n.); pareggiare (vb)*
dribble	*scartare* (to dribble past someone), *dribblare (vb); il dribbling (n.)*
extra time	*i tempi supplementari (n.)*
fan	*il tifoso (n.)*
far post/near post	*il palo lungo/il primo palo (n.)*

final (semi-final, quarter-final)	*la finale (semifinale, quarto di finale) (n.)*
final whistle	*il fischio finale (n.)*
football pitch	*il campo da calcio (n.)*
foul	*fallo (n.);* to commit a foul = *commettere un fallo (vb)*
free kick (direct/indirect)	*il calcio di punizione (diretto/indiretto) (n.)*
friendly	*l'amichevole (n.)*
goal	*il gol (n.); segnare un gol* = to score a goal *(vb);* NB: the physical 'goal' between uprights and crossbar = *la porta (n.)*
goalkeeper	*il portiere (n.)*
goal kick	*il calcio di rinvio (n.)*
half time	*l'intervallo (n.)*
handball	*il fallo di mano (n.);* NB to shout 'handball', use *Mani!* or *arbitro mani!*
hat-trick	*la tripletta (n.);* brace is *la doppietta.*
head the ball, to	*colpire la palla di testa, toccare di testa (vb);* to head the winner = *segnare di testa il gol della vittoria*
injury time	*il recupero (n.);* three minutes' injury time = *tre minuti di recupero*
kick-off	*il calcio d'inizio (n.)*
kick	*il calcio (n.), calciare (vb)*
left back/right back	*il terzino sinistro/destro (n.)*
linesman	*l'assistente arbitro (n.)* (assistant referee), *il guardalinee, il quarto uomo* (fourth official)
lose	*perdere (vb)*
man on!	*occhio!* or *uomo!*
manager/coach/boss (of a national team)	*il CT (n.)* (also written *ct,* or *citì: 'il commissario tecnico'); l'allenatore* is a more general term, used of the coach of any team; a trainer can be addressed as *mister* and is sometimes referred to as *il mister.*
mark	*marcare (vb);* NB: *la difesa a zona/a uomo* = zonal/man-to-man marking
match, game of football	*la partita (n.),* or *l'incontro (n.)*
match (home/away)	*la partita (in casa/in trasferta) (n.)*
midfield	*il centrocampo (n.)*

midfielder (central/left-sided/right-sided)	*il centrocampista (centrale/di sinistra/di destra) (n.)* NB also *il mediano (di interdizione)* = defensive midfield ballwinner; *il regista* = literally '(film) director' – the midfield general who 'runs' a game.
net, the	*la rete (n.)*; NB: *rete* also means 'goal' in the sense of having scored one: *segnare un rete (vb)*
offside	*il fuorigioco (n.)*; to be offside = *essere in fuorigioco*
own goal	*l'autogol/autorete (n.)*; to score an own goal = *fare autogol (vb)*
pass	*il passaggio (n.)*; *passare il pallone (vb)* = to pass the ball
penalty	*il calcio di rigore (n.)*; also simply *il rigore*
penalty area	*l'area di rigore (n.)*
penalty shoot out	*i tiri di rigore (n.)*
pitch	*il campo da gioco (n.)*
player	*il giocatore (n.)*
push up!	*tutti avanti!* or *salire!*
red card/yellow card	*il cartellino rosso/cartellino giallo (n.)*; to get a red/yellow card = *prendere il cartellino rosso/giallo (n.)*
referee	*l'arbitro (n.)*
sack	*l'esonero (n.)*; to sack = *esonerare*
save	*la parata (n.); che parata!* = what a save!; you may also hear *miracolo!* – a 'miracle' save of the Banks vs Pele order
score, to	*segnare* (see also 'net')
send off	*espellere*, past participle: *espulso (vb); l'espulsione (n.)* = a sending off
shoot	*tirare (vb)*
striker	*il centravanti (n.)* = centre forward; *il fantasista* = creative player in the 'hole' e.g. Totti, Del Piero; you will also hear *il goleador, il cannoniere, il bomber*
substitution	*la sostituzione (n.)*; to substitute = *sostituire*
teammate	*il compagno di squadra (n.)*
throw in	*la rimessa laterale (n.)*
win	*la vittoria (n.) vincere (vb)*
wingback (left/right)	*il terzino destro/sinistro (n.)*
World Cup	*la Coppa del Mondo (n.)*